STUCK

MEGAN TWYCROSS

CURRENCY PRESS
The performing arts publisher

CURRENT THEATRE SERIES

First published in 2026
by Currency Press Pty Ltd,
Gadigal Land, Suite 310, 46–56 Kippax Street, Surry Hills, NSW 2010, Australia
enquiries@currency.com.au
www.currency.com.au

in association with La Mama Theatre

Typeset by Brighton Gray for Currency Press.

Printed by Fineline Print + Copy Services, Revesby.
Cover design by Mathias Johannson for Currency Press.
Cover Image Darren Gill, courtesy of La Mama.

Currency Press acknowledges the Traditional Owners of the Country on which we live and work. We pay our respects to all Aboriginal and Torres Strait Islander Elders, past and present.

A catalogue record for this
book is available from the
National Library of Australia

Contents

STUCK was first produced by La Mama at La Mama HQ, Melbourne, on the lands of the Boon Wurrung and Wurundjeri Woi Wurrung peoples of the Kulin Nation, on 6 May 2026 with the following cast:

OLD ONE	Caroline Lee
YOUNG ONE	Eva Seymour

Director, Susie Dee
Producer, Kate Hancock
Set and Costume Designer, Lindy Macauley
Composer, Ian Moorhead
Lighting Designer, Amelia Lever-Davidson

CHARACTERS

OLD ONE. Female, fifty-something.

YOUNG ONE. Female, mid–late teens.

SET

A supermarket deli.

TIME

Now.

NOTE

As events transpire the characters become as violent as they are tender with each other. The breaks between scenes are just as important as the scenes themselves. There is a deli bell. It dings throughout the play.

This playtext went to press before the end of rehearsals and may differ from the play as performed.

1.

The first day.

OLD ONE: Righto, so this is how you cut salami. You get it nice and thin, right?

YOUNG ONE: Right.

OLD ONE: Don't wanna make it too fat, the customers will come back and complain, particularly the old ones. They never like fat salami. Got it?

YOUNG ONE: Got it.

OLD ONE: Never touch the meat with your fingernails, right? Always get your gloves or a plastic bag. 'Kay?

YOUNG ONE: 'Kay.

OLD ONE: Now, if you don't know what to do, don't just stand there looking like a Goodfornuthin. What you gotta do is find The List.

YOUNG ONE: The List?

OLD ONE: The List.

YOUNG ONE: Where's The List?

OLD ONE: Dunno.

YOUNG ONE: Dunno?

OLD ONE: You'll be right.

YOUNG ONE: Right.

OLD ONE: You sure?

YOUNG ONE: Yes, I'm sure.

OLD ONE: Well, what you waiting for Goodfornuthin? What you think I'm paying you for? Get to work.

YOUNG ONE: Righto.

2.

YOUNG ONE: It's cold.

OLD ONE: Quit whinging Goodfornuthin.

YOUNG ONE: Freezing.

OLD ONE: Fridge is stuffed. Thermostat. You'll get used to it.

YOUNG ONE: When's it getting fixed?

OLD ONE: I dunno.

YOUNG ONE: It's freezing. Hands are blue.

OLD ONE: Toughen up Goodfornuthin.

YOUNG ONE: What I gotta do next?

OLD ONE: Check The List.

YOUNG ONE: The List?

OLD ONE: Yes, The List.

YOUNG ONE: Where's The List?

OLD ONE: How many times I gotta tell you? I don't know. Find it yourself. What am I? Mum?

YOUNG ONE: Don't got no mum.

OLD ONE: Oh well, you'll be right. It'll toughen your shell, it will.

YOUNG ONE: She gone a died when I was only a pidderpadder.

OLD ONE: Oh boo-hoo-hoo. I s'pose you think you're special? Well, guess what? I don't got no mum either. You're not special, you're just like everyone else. 'Kay?

YOUNG ONE: 'Kay. Sorry.

OLD ONE: Sorry?

YOUNG ONE: Sorry I said anything.

OLD ONE: The world don't owe you nothing. You gotta get on with things. That's what we all do, bury all that mucky mess and move on.

YOUNG ONE: I'm aiming higher than that. I'm aiming *way* higher! I'm just getting dollars in the bank and I'm outta here.

OLD ONE: Oh yeah, Goodfornuthin? Where you think you're going?

YOUNG ONE: Away. Outta here. Gone.

OLD ONE: So, you're one of those, one of those that think they're betta than the rest of us? I'm happy, I am. I'm happy with me lot and don't you forget it. Right?

YOUNG ONE: Right.

OLD ONE: Got it?

YOUNG ONE: Got it.

OLD ONE: You sure?

YOUNG ONE: Yeah, yeah, I'm sure. It's cold.

OLD ONE: Jeez, well start moving. Get moving about.

YOUNG ONE: Righto righto.

OLD ONE: Get back to work, or your bones will get the laze about them.

3.

YOUNG ONE: Gonna be a something. Gonna be famous, smart, beautiful. Gonna be a flight attendant and spend hours in the sky. Gonna travel round the world in a plane bigger than this here supermarket. Gonna get a good job and buy a house with a slanty roof. I'm going somewhere. Won't be slicing and dicing. Smell freedom and now I'm just saving dollars in the bank and I'm outta here.

I'm just putting up with *her* till I'm gone. All she says is [*as Old One*] *Seeyalater Goodfornuthin. Do this Goodfornuthin. Cut this Goodfornuthin. Doing it wrong Goodfornuthin. Don't need this Goodfornuthin. You know what you want Goodfornuthin? You know what you want? You want pidderpadder. You want a family van with a sliding door. That's what you want Goodfornuthin.*

4.

OLD ONE: You know what you want? You know what you want? You want pidderpadder. You want a family van with a sliding door. Had four of the little beauties, I did. Birthed them right here in this town, I did. Right round the corner. Bought the baby mush for their little mouths right here in this here supermarket. Came through those doors, trakky dacks on, vagina throbbing like an old oyster. T-shirt dripping like a cleaning rag. Got their dummies and their nappies and their wip-ies, all of it, right here. Couldn't be happier all of them.

YOUNG ONE: How'd you know you wanted all that?

OLD ONE: Cos, everyone wants it.

YOUNG ONE: Do they?

OLD ONE: What a stupid question Goodfornuthin. Course they do. Don't know what you want, do you? Pidderpadder will sort that out.

YOUNG ONE: Think so?

OLD ONE: Know so.

YOUNG ONE: What's it feel like? To have something in you like that?

OLD ONE: Depends on who you are and how it got there, doesn't it?

YOUNG ONE: Yeah, s'pose. But what does it feel like?

OLD ONE: Feel like? You want me to tell you what it feels like?
YOUNG ONE: Yeah, s'pose.
OLD ONE: Feels like this.

OLD ONE *grabs a plastic bag and puts some olives in it. She shakes it.*

YOUNG ONE: Shit.
OLD ONE: Yeah, shit shit.
YOUNG ONE: Shit. Really?
OLD ONE: Yeah, really. Give it a go. Go on.
YOUNG ONE: Righto.

YOUNG ONE *grabs a plastic bag and puts some olives in it. She shakes it.*

Okay. I think I know now.
OLD ONE: And like this too.

OLD ONE *shakes the bag again.*

YOUNG ONE: Really? Like this?

YOUNG ONE *shakes her bag again. It explodes. Olives go everywhere.*

OLD ONE: Not like that Goodfornuthin. You Goodfornuthin. You silly little Goodfornuthin. Always making mistakes. Always mucking up. You're never going anywhere.
YOUNG ONE: Yes I am.
OLD ONE: Oh yeah, we'll see.
YOUNG ONE: I'm gonna travel and get outta here. Six months tops. Dollars in the bank. I'm leaving. I'm getting out and I'm gonna be a flight attendant on a plane somewhere.
OLD ONE: Well, la-di-dah. Aren't you a special Young Thing.

Beat.

YOUNG ONE: It's cold.
OLD ONE: Argh quit your whinging. Always complaining about something.
YOUNG ONE: Well, it is. It's cold, bloody freezing.
OLD ONE: It's just part of the package.
YOUNG ONE: What package?

OLD ONE: Working here.
YOUNG ONE: It's so bloody freezing.
OLD ONE: Stop whining. It's not that bad.
YOUNG ONE: Yes, it is. It's freezing.
OLD ONE: Good for you.
YOUNG ONE: When are the fridges getting fixed?
OLD ONE: I said I dunno. Now stop pontificating and do some slicing.

5.

YOUNG ONE *hides.*

OLD ONE *enters.*

YOUNG ONE *jumps out and scares her.*

YOUNG ONE: Rah!
OLD ONE: Arrrrrgh.

YOUNG ONE *laughs.*

Why? Why? Why you be so cruel?
YOUNG ONE: You should've seen your face. [*Laughing*] Your face, like a smashed capsicum.

She copies OLD ONE*'s face and keeps laughing.*

OLD ONE: Cruelness.
YOUNG ONE: Cruelness? Whatever.
OLD ONE: Don't. Do. It. Again.
YOUNG ONE: At least it passes the time. Why shouldn't I?
OLD ONE: Why?
YOUNG ONE: Yeah, why?
OLD ONE: Because I said so. And in case you haven't realised. I'm the boss.
YOUNG ONE: The boss of what? The boss of this? Well la-di-dah.
OLD ONE: You think you're special?
YOUNG ONE: S'pose I'm not special, am I? S'pose I'm just like everyone else. World don't owe me nothing, I s'pose.
OLD ONE: Nothing.
YOUNG ONE: Dad tried his hardest. Good dad he is. Still trying but he's all about hard work and dollars in the bank. [*As her father*] *What you*

want Young Babe, he says, *what you want, is a job close by, steady, not too stressy, easy dollars in the bank.* He worked here just round the corner his whole life. Simple, happy life he says. That's what life is.

OLD ONE: Smart man, your dad. Level-headed. Smart. Got his priorities tip top. Don't wanna wish for too much. Then you never get hurt. Aim medium, fall medium. Aim high, fall too far and you never come back. Level-headed he is.

YOUNG ONE: Level-headed?

OLD ONE: Yes level-headed. You're a smart one.

YOUNG ONE: I'm a smart Goodfornuthin.

OLD ONE: Using your noggin.

YOUNG ONE: I'm using me noggin.

6.

OLD ONE *and* YOUNG ONE *watch customers go by.*

OLD ONE: Mmm … There she goes, there she goes, watch out for that one, Young Thing. Miss Double Ding.

They watch Miss Double Ding from afar.

Five hundred grams of Champagne Ham for the Champagne Hair. Gotta weigh it just right. Not too much, not too little. Five hundred grams exactly. Gotta grab it from the cool room, freshly sliced.

She takes on her voice, overly posh.

Don't take it from the front counter, you just don't know how long it's been there. Who does she take me for? Comes on a Monday, mid-morning. Every week, with her raised eyebrows and her pastel prints. Ding ding. Watch out for that one.

Shit. She's coming this way.

OLD ONE *fixes herself.*

OLD ONE *serves Miss Double Ding.*

YOUNG ONE *watches on.*

They both watch as she walks away.

YOUNG ONE: Why does she ring the bell like that?

OLD ONE: Because …

YOUNG ONE: Because why?
OLD ONE: Because she's Miss Double Ding.

7.

OLD ONE: Bloody ungrateful most of the time, those pidderpadders. Parasites, suck and drain, first from your womb, then from your teat, then from your soul, then from your bank account. Sure they give back, but not before they rip you and your heart in two. Don't give too much, they expect it. Less giving, less expectating, less breaking of the old throb machine.

Can't give no more. No more left. Dried up. Hair limp. Skin saggy. Flabby front bum. Catch meself in the stainless steel and don't know who's staring back. Stopped looking now. Customers ring the bell and look through me, searching for her. *Fresh Meat*.

8.

A busy time on shift.

OLD ONE: [*calling out*] Oi. Need some help. Too busy!
YOUNG ONE: [*from out the back*] Coming!
OLD ONE: C'mon! It's flat chat out here.
YOUNG ONE: Hang on! I'm coming.
OLD ONE: What are you doing?
YOUNG ONE: I said, hang on.
OLD ONE: Hurry up Goodfornuthin! You're slower than an old lady ordering her honey ham.

YOUNG ONE *finally enters.*

YOUNG ONE: Jeez, what's the rush?
OLD ONE: Don't toy with me!

They work.

YOUNG ONE: Flat chat out here.
OLD ONE: What? Too much for you Goodfornuthin?
YOUNG ONE: All good.
OLD ONE: Busy. Good for you. Just gotta get something from out the back.

She begins to leave.

YOUNG ONE: Hey! Where are you going?
OLD ONE: Gotta find The List.
YOUNG ONE: Don't leave me here! I'll never get out by knock-off time.
OLD ONE: You'll be right, if you work quick enough you will, good for you Fresh Meat.
YOUNG ONE: No I won't.
OLD ONE: Yeah you will. Chop chop.

9.

YOUNG ONE *hides.*

OLD ONE *enters and walks past her.*

YOUNG ONE *jumps out and scares her.*

YOUNG ONE: Rah!
OLD ONE: Ahhhhhh!

YOUNG ONE *laughs.*

What the? In the name of … For the love of! Young Thing! I nearly lost me lunch. What have I said? Don't be doing that kind of thing.
YOUNG ONE: Why not?
OLD ONE: Why not?
YOUNG ONE: Yeah, why not?
OLD ONE: It's not professional, it's not right.
YOUNG ONE: Professional? Professional? This place is not professional.
OLD ONE: Watch your words. It is professional. I could work anywhere, anywhere, but I choose to work here. Every day is a choice, and I choose this.
YOUNG ONE: No you don't. This is not a choice.

A customer walks by.

OLD ONE: Shhhhhh. Shhhhh. Act professional.

They pause together and watch the customer go by.

YOUNG ONE: See, you said so yourself. *Act* professional. Acting, acting, this isn't real. This isn't work.
OLD ONE: And I s'pose the money that buys those sneakers, that's not real? And the money that helps put food in my belly, not real? Oh and these here clothes? Not real?

OLD ONE *pretends to pick apples from an invisible tree.*

YOUNG ONE: What are you doing?

OLD ONE *continues, ignoring her.*

Oi, literally, what are you doing?

OLD ONE: Don't interrupt Miss Highandmighty-Goodfornuthin. I'm busy.

YOUNG ONE: Stop it. It's embarrassing. Stop. They can see you.

They both pause.

They watch the customers go by.

They focus on one customer as he approaches.

OLD ONE: Shit. He's coming this way.

OLD ONE *prepares.*

YOUNG ONE *copies.*

They watch, an air of unease.

YOUNG ONE: I served him last week.

OLD ONE: Did you?

YOUNG ONE: Yep.

OLD ONE: Small tub of pasta salad and three hashbrowns?

OLD ONE: Yep.

OLD ONE: Extra mayo?

YOUNG ONE: Yep.

OLD ONE: Did he make you bend down to the front of the fridge? Did you have to get the ones closest to the glass?

YOUNG ONE: Yep.

OLD ONE: Did your skin tingle as he stared at your name badge, just here?

She points across her breast.

YOUNG ONE: Yep.

OLD ONE: Yeah, watch out for that one.

YOUNG ONE: 'Kay.

They both watch and wait until the male customer has gone.

Beat.

OLD ONE *begins picking her imaginary apples again.*

Don't start that again. Stop it. It's embarrassing.

OLD ONE: Well, sorry I'm soooo embarrassing. This is all beneath you. This is all too much like work for you.

YOUNG ONE: Stop. Stop whatever you're doing. Stop it.

OLD ONE: Well, forgive me as I pick this here invisible money off my glorious invisible money tree. Excuse me while I bathe in the glory of all my riches.

YOUNG ONE: You're so weird. You're so past it. This place has gone and robbed you of your brain.

OLD ONE: Careful Young Thing. Careful what you say. You just wait. You wait until you become just, like, me. BOO!

YOUNG ONE: I'm never gonna be like that. Never gonna be like you.

10.

A new day.

YOUNG ONE *enters hurriedly.*

YOUNG ONE: Shit. Shit. Shit. Feeling sick. Feeling sick in the pit of my guts. Gonna vom … Gonna be …

She vomits.

OLD ONE: Jeez, what you doing Fresh Meat? You been out on the piss last night?

YOUNG ONE: No. Nah.

OLD ONE: Bloody hell! At least do it out the back Goodfornuthin, the customers don't need their potato salad with any extra cheese. Disgusting.

YOUNG ONE *vomits again.*

Get your hair out of it. Bloody young things thinking they can get on it midweek. You're an idiot.

YOUNG ONE: Sorry.

OLD ONE: Yeah, well so am I. Bloody hell.

YOUNG ONE: Thanks.

OLD ONE: In our day, at least we did it on the weekend and that was it.

YOUNG ONE: I haven't been drinking.

OLD ONE: That bloody lolly water still has alcohol in it you dafty. I'm gonna have to let the boss know, I think.

YOUNG ONE: I said I haven't been drinking. Promise.

OLD ONE: Well, you had some dodgy prawns. You didn't take the ones from the bottom of the fridge, did you? We all know you don't buy them from the supermarket deli, not the freshest choice, so to speak.

YOUNG ONE: No. No, I …

OLD ONE: Oh, oh! I know what your problem is. Oh, yeah, I know … Can't believe I didn't see it before. Jeez Old One, you bloody moron. I can see it from here. Come to think of it, I saw it as you went through those auto doors this morning. You look different. Your skin's all oily. You got bags under your eyes and your chicken breasts are looking a mighty bit fuller! Ding! You up-the-duff. Ding! You gone and changed your life forever. Ding! Goodfornuthin you're a Goodforsomethin now. You fresh young thing. You're a bloody Goodforsomethin! You better go to Aisle Nine and get yourself a piss stick. Get a few, and some pills. And Aisle Three for some greasy chips. Holy bloody moly. You all sprogged up! Bloody Fresh Meat.

YOUNG ONE: No. No, I'm not.

OLD ONE: Oh yes you are. Silly young thing.

YOUNG ONE: Nah I'm not. No! I'm getting outta here, I'm going places. I'm leaving here for good. Just working for some cash, dollars in the bank. The deal was six months tops and, and for a car and I'll see you later. See you all later … Oh, gonna, be—

She vomits.

OLD ONE: You're not going anywhere but Aisle Nine and the doctors Fresh Meat. Bet you wished you had a mum now. Don't know what you're gonna do without her. What you think of this little pitted olive? Hope The Sperm in all of this is the type to stick round? Is he? The type? Not many of them are.

YOUNG ONE: Dunno.

OLD ONE: Well, is he? Is he the type to stick around?

YOUNG ONE: I said I dunno.

OLD ONE: Well, I've never met him.

YOUNG ONE: Maybe there's a reason for that.

OLD ONE: Oh, you think you're so much better than all of us, don't you?

YOUNG ONE: No, I don't. I just wanna go do something a bit, a bit …

OLD ONE: A bit?

YOUNG ONE: A bit. Different.

OLD ONE: Yeah well. You never knew much, did ya Goodfornuthin?

YOUNG ONE: I did. I do. I feel shithouse.

OLD ONE: It passes.

YOUNG ONE: Doesn't feel like it. Feels like it's gonna go on forever and ever and ever.

OLD ONE: Well, suck it up, it's good for you. You're a Goodforsomethin now.

YOUNG ONE: What you mean a Goodforsomethin? How come?

OLD ONE: How come? How come?

YOUNG ONE: How come I wasn't a Goodforsomethin to start with?

OLD ONE: Just cos.

YOUNG ONE: Cos why?

OLD ONE: Well, because you're a Goodforsomethin now. 'Kay?

YOUNG ONE: 'Kay. Feel shit. Hands are blue.

OLD ONE: Go and warm them on the chickens. Or find The List.

YOUNG ONE: The List?

OLD ONE: Yeah, The List. That'll keep you busy, warm you up.

YOUNG ONE: Can't we fix the fridges?

OLD ONE: What have I said Fresh Meat. What have I said?

YOUNG ONE: It's out of your control.

OLD ONE: It's out of my control Fresh Meat. I don't know when those bloody tradies are gonna come and fix the fridges.

YOUNG ONE: What am I gonna do?

OLD ONE: What we all do.

YOUNG ONE: What's that?

OLD ONE: Have babies, cut salami, sell chicken loaf. You'll be right.

YOUNG ONE: Feel shit. Feel shit shit shit.

11.

OLD ONE: Birthed all four of them out of me. None of this slice and dice shit.

She talks as if to the doctor.

Stand back Doc. I got this. Stand back. I said stand back! You ever birth one of these? Have you?! No. Well what did I say. Push off and let me take care of things.

With the first one, thought I'd go to heaven I did. Be off with the Mother Angels, be in their care, step out of my flesh and watch down from the sky. Bah! What was that? Life, you lie. Women, you lie. Remember every bloody thing. Every bloody thing four times. Four times over, I remember.

Birth, that's the easy bit. Piss easy. Takes care of itself. Raising them takes the guts. Cos of them I've got bags for eyes, bags for tits, bags for butt cheeks. And now, now, sometimes I think my flaps are so far gone they're gonna whistle in the wind.

Their *Father* left me, didn't he? He took one last look at me over his shoulder and walked out. Yeah, well good riddance, so what if he went and left me for someone younger. Fresher. Tighter. So what?

But you know what? Proud. Proud I am. Proud of what I've done. I worked hard. I even learnt how to deal with that government chit chat for money. I got good at that. [*As if to her children.*] Righto kids, shine up nice and bright, time for the chit chat. [*Whining like children*] *Don't wanna Mum*, they say, *don't wanna Mum*, they say, *do we have to?* They say, and I say, [*to her children*] *Yes you do have to. You got to. You got to or we don't eat nothing till next week. Now shut it!* Still good at it, if you don't mind me saying so.

YOUNG ONE *interrupts.*

YOUNG ONE: Good at what?

OLD ONE: All that government chit chat. Centrelink.

YOUNG ONE: Never gonna do that. Never gonna freeload.

OLD ONE: Hey, I'm no freeloader. Who says I don't work hard? I work bloody hard, bloody hard my whole life.

YOUNG ONE: And you still need to get that government money?

OLD ONE: Who said that all that talking to The Government isn't just like working a job? You could say I've worked two jobs. You ever talked to them?

YOUNG ONE: Who?

OLD ONE: The Government?

YOUNG ONE: Nah.

OLD ONE: Well get ready, now you're expecting a pidderpadder. Get ready to fill out those forms. Get a password. Lose a password. Register it. Get another password. Bloody hell. With the time it takes it could be a full-time job.

YOUNG ONE: Whatever.

OLD ONE: Well I'm proud. I'm proud and don't you forget it. Cos of me, my little beauties grew up nice and strong. Cos of me, me kids grew up eating leftover little boys with sauce for dinner, strass and sauce in white bread for lunch, kraft and kabana, twiggy sticks for snacks. Should see them now. Bloody strapping the lot of them. And me, proud as, proud of what I've done.

12.

YOUNG ONE: Feeling cold. Feeling numb. *Do* know The Sperm in all this. Know him and know it's the last thing I wanna think about forever and ever and ever. He changed me. Changed me forever. Don't wanna think about it. He robbed me of my soul and turned my heart to gristle.

My first time, my first time I was gonna be taken away with the pleasure angels. It was gonna be the most special thing. I'd be looking down on me and him from the sky. From a dreamy white cloud, like a god or an angel. We'd lie there forever and ever, touching, stroking, nuzzling, even nibbling, gently. Here or there, or here, or there, or here!

Giggles.

Our hearts would beat as one, they'd beat as one, like this, gagoon, gagoon, gagoon and we'd be lost in each other's feathery down, like two little baby chickens. We'd be entwined in sexy exaltation. Yeah, well life, you lie. It was nothing like that, was it?

13.

OLD ONE *hides.*

YOUNG ONE *enters, exhausted, sick.*

OLD ONE *jumps out and scares her.*

YOUNG ONE *reacts.*

OLD ONE: Bloody love this game Fresh Meat! Can't believe I didn't think of it myself.

YOUNG ONE: I think I'm sick of it.

OLD ONE: Sick of it? Sick of it?
YOUNG ONE: Yeah, nah. Tired. Tired of it.
OLD ONE: BOO! Just warming up!
YOUNG ONE: Too cold to warm up, don't you think?
OLD ONE: Nup. Just getting started.
YOUNG ONE: Do you know where The List is?
OLD ONE: When are you going to start fending for yourself Goodfornuthin?
YOUNG ONE: But it's your job to help me. You're the boss.
OLD ONE: Only to a point and I'm afraid, yep, I feel like, yep, today, that point has passed.
YOUNG ONE: Yeah, but I'm so tired and cold, so freezing.
OLD ONE: Here, ding this bell, it'll lift your spirits.

OLD ONE *tries to play a tune on the deli bell.*

YOUNG ONE *puts up with it for a while, then snatches it and puts it back on the counter.*

YOUNG ONE: Home time.

14.

OLD ONE: You look different Fresh Meat, Goodfornuthin. I mean, Goodforsomethin.
YOUNG ONE: Feel better I do.
OLD ONE: Must've come through it.
YOUNG ONE: Come through it?
OLD ONE: You know? Through it.
YOUNG ONE: …
OLD ONE: The first bit, the first few months.
YOUNG ONE: Oh.
OLD ONE: Anyway, got some news.
YOUNG ONE: News?
OLD ONE: Yep. News. The fridges.
YOUNG ONE: The fridges?
OLD ONE: The fridges are gonna get fixed.

15.

YOUNG ONE: I'm throwing on some clothes in the back seat of his car and he's revving the shit out of it. The lights are about to turn green and the beats are pumping. He's checking me out in the rearview mirror but pretending he isn't. He's munching on bits of chicken loaf; the ones I've stolen for him. He looks happy. [*Gruffly*] *Thanks liddle lobster!* He says, *Mmmm chicken loaf, reminds me of me mum. Let me nip ya, let me nip ya, me little lobster, nip nip nip.* Know he isn't much, know it's just a bit of fun, a bit of fun till I get outta here. Know he doesn't love me but being wanted is enough, being wanted is enough for me.

But now? I just wanna, I just wanna tear my flesh off. I wanna peel myself open like a frankfurter and drop my skin in the bin.

16.

OLD ONE: How's that belly?

YOUNG ONE: You know I'm a person too. You can ask me something else. I have a brain! I am more than just what's inside me.

OLD ONE: Touchy!

YOUNG ONE: Ask me something else! Anything else.

OLD ONE: Mooo-dy. That's alright, I'll forgive you, must be your hormones.

YOUNG ONE: Are they coming today?

OLD ONE: Who?

YOUNG ONE: You know.

OLD ONE: No I don't.

YOUNG ONE: Yes you do.

OLD ONE: There's work to be done Fresh Meat, stop messing me about. What is it?

YOUNG ONE: Are the fellas coming to fix the fridges?

OLD ONE: Do you want the long or the short answer?

YOUNG ONE: Stop messing me about. Just give me an answer. You said they were coming.

OLD ONE: Long answer is they've got other engagements. They're over-committed. They're all booked up. [*Like a tradie*] *Can't make it till next month. Sorry missus, we're too busy. Sorry ma'am, we just can't fit youse in.*

YOUNG ONE: But are they coming? You said they were.

OLD ONE: Jeez Goodfornuthin-somethin. You're bloody thick as bocconcini sometimes. No, they're not coming.

YOUNG ONE: What do you mean they're not coming? My hands are blue! My toes are curling like those prawns in the fridge.

OLD ONE: Nah that's the fluid doing that to you. That's cos you gone and got yourself up-the-pork. Don't blame me Goodforsomethin. Blame them tradies. Full of broken promises and wait-till-next-weeks, they are.

YOUNG ONE: You're just like the rest of them. Full of taramasalata. You never booked them, did you?

OLD ONE: Boss said they cost too much. Here, have some socks. Got them from hosiery. Be grateful, I say. That's what everyone says. Gratefulness equals mindfulness equals happiness.

YOUNG ONE: What am I meant to do with these?

OLD ONE: Keeping you warm, you dafty.

YOUNG ONE: You're just like all the rest of them. All of them. Every single one of them. I'm getting outta here, six months tops.

17.

OLD ONE: A miracle. It's a miracle! Here I was thinking I was starting to dry up, my waters all dried up, my uterus all shriveled like a sun-dried tomato. Here I was feeling just a little pang of jealousy, a little seed of hate, of green. The green-eyed monster was swimming in the pit of my guts and now look at me. I can't believe it. I gosh darn can't effing believe it. A diet full of hormone-filled chicken is better than collagen I reckon. Who needs that collagen when you can buy a BBQ chicken for ten-ninety-nine?

I went to the doctor you see. I went to the doctor and I said [*as if to the doctor*] Doc, I'm here for a mid-life checkup. I think it's time that me monthly flows are finally taking a back seat, a different course, you know? It's time that I went through 'the big change'. I'm all hot, then I'm cold, then I'm hot and sheez have I been cranky. Then crying, uncontrollably like my whole life is flowing through me and out my head holes. Crying, crying, crying. Then hot, so hot I have to strip off, right there and then.

She has a hot flush, it's dramatic.

So, he did some tests and you'll never guess it. Here I was thinking I was going through The Big Change, The Big See-ya-later, I was feeling so many feelings, relief, sadness, oldness.

[*As if to the doctor again*] But Doc, what you telling me, what you telling me, is that I'm not going through the end of my cycle? I'm actually, I'm actually, what you mean? What you mean, is that I am actually, is that I'm actually … pregnant?! There is a slight chance that I've got a baby. A baby! I can't be. I can't be. That's out-effin-rageous. I'm a freak. A freak. Too old. Toooo old for that! Surely I'm too old for that. Are you sure? You sure? You're not one hundred percent sure, you're gonna run some more tests, but you think there might be a slight chance that I might be. Don't get too ahead of myself. Don't get too carried away, just wait for the tests, it's highly unlikely, but, but there is a slight chance I *could* be. Well, that's good enough for me!

I'm gonna have a baby! I thought my time was up! I thought my waters were all dried up. But here I am with a second chance. Not that I know how it got there. I certainly haven't been having any rendezvous or hanky pank panky, so maybe I'm not, but Doc thinks that maybe I am. Who knows?

Shit me. What if I'm like that lady in all the books. You know the one. That lady, you know, that lady in all the books that didn't have sex, aww, can't think of her name. You know the one that invented Christmas by pushing outta baby next to a donkey. You know, Martha, nah Margaret. Molly? Was it Molly? Shit me.

18.

OLD ONE: How you feeling Fresh Meat? How's that belly?
YOUNG ONE: Dunno. Trying not to think about it.
OLD ONE: Why not? It's a bloody great thing you got in there.
YOUNG ONE: Is it? Isn't it just the most ordinary thing in the world?

OLD ONE: Nope it's a bloody miracle and don't you ever forget it.

YOUNG ONE: Nah I won't ever forget it. Haunts me like a shadow from the inside.

OLD ONE: Go on, what is it? What's different about me? What do you think? You'll never guess it? Not in a million months will you guess it.

YOUNG ONE: Do I have to?

OLD ONE: C'mon Goodforsomethin. Where's your sparkle?

YOUNG ONE: Too cold to sparkle. Need them fridges fixed.

OLD ONE: Quit your complaining Goodforsomethin! Jeez you're a bore.

YOUNG ONE: Fix them fridges and I might think about it.

OLD ONE: C'mon. Look at me. Look at me. Is there something different?

YOUNG ONE: You got sauce on your face?

OLD ONE: Nah. Something different. Better. Am I radiating? Glowing? Am I sparkling?

YOUNG ONE: Nah.

OLD ONE: C'mon Fresh Meat. Look. Look closer. Look at my lady stomach. My lady bits.

YOUNG ONE: No thanks.

OLD ONE: Not those lady bits! Use your noggin, ding dong. Look at my skin. Do I look younger?

YOUNG ONE: For pork sake! No. Just tell me.

OLD ONE: Your hormones have rubbed off or something. I'm a miracle! I'm like that virgin lady in all the books. I'm gonna have a little milk sucker, a little pidderpadder, just like you. We gonna do it together. We gonna be mummy friends and walk our prams, we gonna talk about our cabbage leaves and our lab-i-as. We gonna wear all that stretchy gear and be BFFs—Best Friends Forever!

YOUNG ONE: Bullshit.

OLD ONE: No bull, no cow, no nothing. It's true, Doctor said so! We're gonna spend our savings on babycinos and go to mumma's group and talk about how gosh-darn-tired we are. Never needed any of that in my day but I'm just happy to be a Goodforsomethin just like you! I'm a Goodforsomethin. I'm a Goodforsomethin just like you. We're gonna be Goodforsomethins together!

YOUNG ONE: Bull bull bull bull bull. You having me on? You're full of it. You're full of it and then some.

OLD ONE: Cross my uterus and hope to die, stick a 'little boy' in my eye. The only thing I'm full of is magical, mythical, mystical sprog. Eight weeks yesterday and counting

YOUNG ONE: But you're old. Look at you. Too old for that shit. You've lost your olives. You've lost it fair and square. [*Calling out*] Doc? Doc? Get this lady a white jacket, it's time she went for a big old rest and a lie down.

OLD ONE: You don't believe me?

YOUNG ONE: Course I don't, you're a looney. You need a new doctor. One that knows what they're doing. One that's for brains, not for *this.*

OLD ONE: This?

YOUNG ONE: Yes, this! That.

OLD ONE: That?

YOUNG ONE: That, that. Whatever that is!

OLD ONE: Watch me. Watch me grow and you'll eat your words! You Goodfornuthin that thinks they know everything cos they're younger than me. You know nothing. You know nothing about anything, about priorities, about life. You just watch. I'm gonna be a mum, doesn't matter how old I am.

And this time it's gonna be different. I'm gonna be a queen! I might even have a little girl. A girl who appreciates her mother and grows up understanding what it is to be a real woman in this world, sacrificing and working and working and working and not ever getting ahead but just being pulled back down, like a crab, into the big old bucket of life!

Now, what's that? What's that sound? Ding! Oh, it's the sound of work. Ding! Oh, here it is again. Ding! Go and clean the fridges and buzz off.

19.

YOUNG ONE: I've been sliced and diced. My heart feels like gristle in my chest. Lady bits are bleeding, for days, weeks. Shouting. Screaming. My guts are screaming. Can't think of nothing else. Nothing.

I never thought I'd be one of those girls. I was always gonna be someone. I worked hard. I was smart. Teachers loved me. I was never one of the cool girls. It's funny that they were called cool. More like drool, or fool. I'm not a fool. But the doctor looks at me like I am, like I am a fool. I want to yell at them. Yell and say I didn't ask for this! I'm not one of those girls, I'm not. Take this alien lobster out of me!

20.

OLD ONE *hides.*

YOUNG ONE *enters and walks past her.*

OLD ONE *jumps out and scares her.*

YOUNG ONE: Don't. Do. That!

OLD ONE: Two can play at this game! You think you're the only one? Just cos I'm old doesn't mean diddly-squat. Oldness doesn't mean you can't have fun and don't you forget it!

YOUNG ONE: It's not like that.

OLD ONE: Just cos I'm old, just cos I have a craggy face and bingo wings? Heh? Heh?

YOUNG ONE: I said, it's not like that.

OLD ONE: Isn't it? You can't see it? The way the customers look through me. Looking for you.

YOUNG ONE: Bull bull bull. You're full of it.

OLD ONE: You just wait. Your turn will come.

YOUNG ONE: What about Only Dodoni? What about him?

OLD ONE: What about him?

YOUNG ONE: He only wants you. He always asks for you.

OLD ONE: Bull bull bull.

YOUNG ONE: It's true. He's told me it's the way you *cut it.*

OLD ONE: You having me on.

YOUNG ONE: No, I'm not and I don't think it's just the way you *cut it.*

OLD ONE: Well, he has been coming in for a long time. We're just acquaintances.

YOUNG ONE: He could choose any supermarket in town, but he doesn't, he chooses this one.

OLD ONE: He lives up the road Fresh Meat. No more reason than that.

YOUNG ONE: Bull bull bull.

OLD ONE: No, no bull.

YOUNG ONE: I think it's more than what you're letting on. I think you're more than *acquaintances*. Watch out for that one.

She winks.

OLD ONE: Nope. No. It wouldn't be proper.

YOUNG ONE: Proper? Proper? When have you ever been proper?

OLD ONE: You know nothing. Nothing.

YOUNG ONE: I know enough about life to know that whatever you got in there, if it really is what you say it is, if it is, it had to get there somehow.

OLD ONE: Yeah, well Only Dodoni would be punching above his weight if he thought he could get his hands on this craggy face and these here bingo wings. I'm a miracle, remember? So there.

YOUNG ONE: Whatever.

21.

Clanging noises can be heard.

OLD ONE: Young Thing! What the heck are you doing?

Clanging continues.

Fresh Meat!

YOUNG ONE *enters with a tool in her hand.*

Not working too hard are you? We gotta look after ourselves, don't we?

YOUNG ONE: Well, you'll be proud, you'll be proud of what I've done!

OLD ONE: What are you doing?

YOUNG ONE: Today's the day. Six months today. I've been here for six months and I'm taking things into my own hands.

OLD ONE: What are you on about?

YOUNG ONE: I'm fixing things. I'm fixing those fridges. I've educated myself on the ways of the thermostat and I'm fixing things.

OLD ONE: But that's not your job. That's not what I'm, or the boss, is paying you for.

YOUNG ONE: Yeah, but I, we, can't do my, our, job unless we fix them. So here I am fixing them.

OLD ONE: Nup. Nup, nup, nup.

YOUNG ONE: What are you on about?

OLD ONE: Nup.

She steals the tool and throws it away.

YOUNG ONE: Hey!

OLD ONE: This is not your job. *Your* job is to sell ham and clean fridges and do it with a smile! I am not paying you for this!

YOUNG ONE: Bull. I'm showing initiative. I'm being useful.

OLD ONE: Nup. Won't have it. Won't. Go find The List. That's your job.

YOUNG ONE: No.

OLD ONE: Yes.

YOUNG ONE: No. You can't make me.

OLD ONE: Yes. I. Can. Get back to your job. The one I am paying you for.

YOUNG ONE: Paying me? *You're* not paying me.

OLD ONE: Don't give me lip. You won't have a job. You won't have a job, and you won't have any money and then where will you be?

YOUNG ONE: Well, maybe I'll get another job. I'm smart, I can do things.

YOUNG ONE *goes to get the tool.* OLD ONE *stands in her way.*

OLD ONE: But are you? Are you smart? Doesn't really matter if you're smart, it matters if you've got money and without this job, you got none of that, none of it.

YOUNG ONE: I'm sick of this.

YOUNG ONE *takes off her apron, ready to leave.*

OLD ONE: Go on then. Leave. It's six months today. Go on! You think the world will be kind? You think it will be kind to a young mum with nothing? Ha. Bloody useless you are. Why don't you just listen. I know. I know things. I know how this world works and it's gonna eat you up like the little chicken thigh you are.

YOUNG ONE *continues to leave but with hesitation.*

Go on! Get outta here Miss La-di-dah! What? Scared? You scared?

YOUNG ONE *is on the verge of leaving but for some reason she can't.*

See. I knew it. Knew you didn't have it in you!

YOUNG ONE: Yeah, well I will. Just not today, not today.

22.

OLD ONE: Phew. Been busy today Goodforsomethin. My feet feel heavier than a bag of ice. All swollen they are. How's your legs? How's your feet? Tired? So tired. Bloody kids, eh? Eh?

Not chatting today. Not feeling like using that tongue of yours. Fair enough, all that energy going into growing our wee babes, I think.

Oh, you should've seen me. When my friends asked me. Should've seen me answer their questions. Yes Berryl, I'm the modern-day virgin. Yes, Shaz, it's a bloody miracle. Yes, it's me. Knew I'd be a special one day I did. Yes Shirl, I'm old but I still got it! I can still grow a little one. Yes, I do feel like her, that lady with the donkey. Meredith, Maisie, how come it's so bloody hard to remember her …

YOUNG ONE: Mary! It's Mary! And you're not growing a baby. You're telling porkies and don't you forget it. The doctor said it was a maybe, a *big* maybe, you just can't handle that you're drying up!

OLD ONE: Porkies? Porkies? I'll pork you! Twenty weeks yesterday and don't you forget it.

YOUNG ONE: Liar! If you're twenty weeks where's the bump? Where's the proof? Show me. Show me.

OLD ONE: Well, where's your proof? You show me. Where's your bump? I'll show you mine if you show me yours. Show me.

YOUNG ONE: No.

OLD ONE: Show me.

YOUNG ONE: Can't.

OLD ONE: Show me. Show me. [*Escalating*] What? Crayfish got your tongue? Show me Goodfornuthin.

YOUNG ONE: No.

OLD ONE: [*violently*] Show me!

YOUNG ONE: You wanna? You really wanna know? You don't know nothing. You don't know nothing about life. You stand there pontificating, so pious and mighty. You don't know nothing.

OLD ONE: Just show me.

YOUNG ONE: Here. Look.

She shows her belly, it's completely flat.

Nothing.

Nothing there.

OLD ONE *is silent.*

OLD ONE: Young One. What you done? What you done?

YOUNG ONE: None of your business. It's no-one's business. Not yours. Not anyone's.

OLD ONE: But you and me, we be …

YOUNG ONE: We be nothing.

OLD ONE: But you and me …

YOUNG ONE: We be nothing.

OLD ONE: But where is it Young One?

YOUNG ONE: It's none of your business.

OLD ONE: But. Where. Is. It?!

YOUNG ONE: It's no-one's business. Leave me alone.

OLD ONE: But I don't understand.

YOUNG ONE: Are you thick? Are you dumb? I'm thick as bocconcini? You're thick as that freezer wall! It's in a bin. It's in a bin, in the deep dark guts of a hospital somewhere. Somewhere I never have to think about it ever ever again.

OLD ONE *is silent.*

OLD ONE: But you and me …

YOUNG ONE: We be nothing. We be nothing.

23.

OLD ONE: Every day she comes in. Every day. She asks [*as a frail old European lady*] *Three hundred grams of Jarlsberg and a tub of hummus*. She comes in with her walker, left wheel squeaking, wrists shaking, a vacant stare. The only outing for her day. Her fleecy-pilly tracksuit and her Hush Puppies. Dunno if I ever wanna wear something like that. Ever.

With my uniform. I'm something. Someone. I got priorities. I'm busy. Never gonna be like Three-hundred-grams-of-Jarlsberg-and-a-tub-of-hummus. She's got no-one, except us, and who are we to her?

Don't even know her name.

OLD ONE *holds her stomach.*

24.

OLD ONE *stands next to* YOUNG ONE *and breathes through her pain as* YOUNG ONE *speaks.*

YOUNG ONE: I'm on the road. In a car, with nothing but me and the steering wheel. Or in the ocean, on a boat with nothing but space and I can breathe. Or flying in the sky, flying like a bird, like an aeroplane … just me.

I breathe so deep that my lungs feel like they're gonna explode into tiny fragments. My lungs burst like a feel-good firework and there's no-one telling me this, or that, or this or that. There's no noise. No noise drowning nothing out. Silence. Just me.

OLD ONE *keels over in pain and grabs her stomach.*

25.

OLD ONE: Still can't believe you gone and done that.

YOUNG ONE: Leave me alone. I don't owe you nothing.

OLD ONE: Thought you were someone different, didn't I? Thought you were better than that.

YOUNG ONE: What makes you an expert on anything? Leave me alone.

Beat.

What I gotta do next?

OLD ONE: …

YOUNG ONE: Where's The List?

OLD ONE: …

YOUNG ONE: Fine. I'll do it myself.

26.

OLD ONE: Happy Anniversary.

YOUNG ONE: What?

OLD ONE: Twelve months today.

YOUNG ONE: How'd you know that?

OLD ONE: I've been counting. I've been watching.

YOUNG ONE: Watching?

OLD ONE: Watching you melt away. You're not trying hard enough.

YOUNG ONE: I am, I am. I work hard.

OLD ONE: No. Not that. You need to try harder.

YOUNG ONE: But I am. I'm trying.

OLD ONE: Try harder.

YOUNG ONE: I am.

OLD ONE: Really?

YOUNG ONE: I apply. I write resumes. I put myself out there. I knock on doors. I've done an interview.

OLD ONE: One interview?

YOUNG ONE: They didn't want me. Said I was too young. Didn't have enough experience. I don't get it. I'm there to *get* experience.

OLD ONE: Only one interview. You gotta try harder than that.

YOUNG ONE: But.

OLD ONE: Excuses!

YOUNG ONE: But I don't know anyone out there, I don't have connections. I'm nothing. I go out there and I try and try and they just look through me. I'm invisible. I'm nothing to them. It's all about who you know and how you know them. And I got no-one. No-one wants someone like me.

OLD ONE: Gonna give up then?

YOUNG ONE: But I'm nothing. I'm nothing out there.

OLD ONE: Well, you're nothing in here, so what does that tell you?

YOUNG ONE: I'm a piece of shit.

OLD ONE: No. That tells me you gotta try harder.

27.

YOUNG ONE *alone in the deli.*

She is cold.

She is tired.

She is isolated.

YOUNG ONE: Catch myself in the stainless steel and dunno who's staring back.

OLD ONE *holds her belly.*

Scene 28 takes place over an extended period of time as the store closes and the deli gets colder. The breaks (28A, 28B, etc.) indicate time passing and a distinct shift in mood.

28A.

YOUNG ONE *hides. It's her best spot yet.*

OLD ONE *enters.*

YOUNG ONE *scares her.*

OLD ONE *screams like she's never screamed before.*

OLD ONE: MARY MOTHER OF GOD!
YOUNG ONE*:* [*laughing*] Got you good. Got you so good.
OLD ONE*:* [*laughing along*] So funny …

Morphs into pain.

… ahhh
YOUNG ONE: Got you so good. Smashed Capsicum.
OLD ONE: Ahh, my back, my bits … [*Holding her stomach*] argh …
YOUNG ONE: Old One?
OLD ONE: Ahhhh.
YOUNG ONE: You okay?
OLD ONE: I dunno. It bloody hurts … ahhhh.
YOUNG ONE: Shit. What are we gonna do?
OLD ONE: Ahhhh. World, why you be so cruel?
YOUNG ONE: We gotta go to the hospital.
OLD ONE: Nah way Fresh Meat. Nah way. We're not going anywhere. Those docs look at me. They look at me like I don't know nothing. They look me up and down with their olive-pip eyes.

YOUNG ONE *goes to help her.*

Stand back, I got this! Plus, the pastrami needs slicing and the loaf needs weighing.
YOUNG ONE: But you're, you're …
OLD ONE: No. Slice that pastrami!
YOUNG ONE: But?
OLD ONE: Weigh that loaf!

OLD ONE *stands behind the deli counter. Blood begins to ooze from under it.*

YOUNG ONE: Fark! Old One!

OLD ONE: What? What?

YOUNG ONE: Bleeding! You're bleeding!

OLD ONE: Too old. Nothing can be done.

YOUNG ONE: Nothing?

OLD ONE: Nothing.

28B.

OLD ONE: I'm scared Young One. I'm scared like no-one been scared in their whole life.

YOUNG ONE: Whatever you're doing. It's scary business.

OLD ONE: I'm scared.

YOUNG ONE: You'll be okay. You'll be right. You said so.

Blood continues to puddle and grow.

OLD ONE: Help me?

YOUNG ONE: You want me to help you?

OLD ONE: Yes. I want you. No-one else.

YOUNG ONE: But you got family. You got people.

OLD ONE: Help me.

YOUNG ONE: But you got your people.

OLD ONE: No. I don't. I got no-one. No-one.

YOUNG ONE: You lie.

OLD ONE: No-one wants someone like me.

YOUNG ONE: Someone wants someone like you. Promise.

OLD ONE: Promise? Promise? I doubt it. No-one ever kept a promise in the history of life.

YOUNG ONE: I will. I will.

OLD ONE: No you won't. You won't. You be a liar just like everyone.

YOUNG ONE: No I'm not, I'm not.

OLD ONE: Why don't you just leave? What's keeping you here? You got enough money, enough savings, go on, get!

YOUNG ONE: But you said you needed me. You said I wouldn't cope. You said I'm a chicken thigh.

OLD ONE: Get. Outta here.

YOUNG ONE: But …

Blood continues to ooze.

28C.

OLD ONE: You know what? I'm freezing. I never felt the cold, you know. Never felt it. I just got used to it. I just got on with it, and now, suddenly, I can feel it. I can feel it in my bones. I'm cold, so cold. I'm just like you now Fresh Meat. We can be cold together.

They shiver together for a moment.

Blood continues to ooze.

YOUNG ONE: Can't feel many things.

OLD ONE: Not many, no.

YOUNG ONE: Be better that way, not feeling things.

OLD ONE: I should've let you fix them fridges.

YOUNG ONE: Yeah, but you said it yourself. Not my job.

OLD ONE: Yeah, but now, numb.

YOUNG ONE: Numb.

OLD ONE: Yes, numb.

YOUNG ONE: Bloody look at us, would you?

OLD ONE: Looking. I'm looking. Don't see much. Do you?

YOUNG ONE: No nothing.

OLD ONE: Yeah nothing.

OLD ONE *starts to disappear.*

YOUNG ONE: Used to see stuff.

OLD ONE: Used to see stuff. Better this way.

YOUNG ONE: Yeah, much better this way.

OLD ONE: Yeah, much better.

OLD ONE *fades into oblivion.*

Silence.

28D.

YOUNG ONE *looks towards the door. As if she might escape. Leave forever.*

She doesn't.

29.

YOUNG ONE: Right, so this is how you cut salami. You get it nice and thin, right? Right. Don't wanna make it too fat, the customers will come back and complain, particularly the old ones. They never like fat salami. Got it? Got it. Never touch the meat with your fingernails, right? Right. Always get your gloves or a plastic bag. 'Kay? 'Kay. Now, if you don't know what to do, don't just stand there looking like a Goodfornuthin, what you gotta do is find The List.

The List.

THE END

presents

STUCK

by
Megan Twycross

6-24 May, 2026

ACTOR **Caroline Lee**
ACTOR **Eva Seymour**

Director **Susie Dee**
Producer **Kate Hancock**
Set and costume designer **Lindy Macauley**
Composer **Ian Moorhead**
Lighting designer **Amelia Lever-Davidson**

STUCK has been supported by the Victorian Government through Creative Victoria, Regional Arts Fund, Regional Arts Victoria, the Fletcher Jones Family Foundations and the Robert Salzer Foundation.

STUCK was first written in 2020 and had a moved reading with the support of Warrnambool Theatre Company. The work was selected for development through La Mama's Explorations program in 2024 and received further development through the La Mama Residency Program in 2025.

CEO & Artistic Director
Caitlin Dullard

General Manager
Julian Dibley-Hall

Pathways & Partnerships Manager
Myf Powell

Marketing & Communications Manager
Georgina Capper

Ticketing & FOH Manager
Gemma Horbury

Venue & Technical Manager
Shane Grant

Producer (Education) & School Publication Coordinator
Maureen Hartley

Producer (First Nations)
Glenn Shea

Producer (Digital)
Ruiqi Fu

Producer (La Mama Presents, Fringe)
Nicki Jam

Producer (Festivals, FaraDays)
Dora Abraham

Curators
Gemma Horbury (Musica); **Amanda Anastasi** (Poetica); **Isabel Knight** (Cabaretica); **Emma Fawcett** (La Mama Scratch)

Documentation
Darren Gill

La Mama Theatre is on traditional land of the people of the Kulin Nation. We give our respect to the Elders of these traditional lands, and to all First Nations people, past and present, and future. We acknowledge all events take place on stolen lands and that sovereignty was never ceded.

FRONT OF HOUSE STAFF

Staff, plus Laurence Strangio, Andreas Petropoulos, Dennis Coard, Susan Bamford Caleo, Penelope Efstathiou, Tony Song, Dani Hayek, Yogashree.

COMMITTEE OF MANAGEMENT

La Mama is financially assisted by Creative Australia, Creative Victoria and the Robert Salzer Foundation.

We are grateful to all our philanthropic partners and donors, advocates, volunteers, audiences, artists and our entire community. Thank you!

La Mama Theatre and Office is at:
205 Faraday St Carlton VIC 3053
La Mama Courthouse Theatre, 349 Drummond Street, Carlton VIC 3053
www.lamama.com.au | email: info@lamama.com.au
Facebook: lamama.theatre | Instagram: lamamatheatre
Office phone 03 9347 6948
Office Mon–Fri, 11am–6pm, Sun 11am–4pm

STANDING OVATION FOR AUSTRALIA'S HOME FOR INDEPENDENT THEATRE

In 2026, La Mama celebrates 59 years of nurturing new Australian Theatre, fearlessly facilitating independent theatre making.

La Mama's Vision is to spark a theatre of possibility, creating life-changing moments which transform individuals and shape the future of Australian storytelling.

La Mama's Mission is to empower artists, audience and art-making.

Built in 1883 for Anthony Reuben Ford, a Carlton printer, the original building in Faraday Street had been used as a workshop, a boot and shoe factory, an electrical engineering workshop and a silk underwear factory before becoming a theatre in 1967. It was established by Betty Burstall and modelled on the experimental off-off-Broadway coffee house theatre activities in New York's Greenwich Village, the centrepiece of which was Ellen Stewart's thriving La MaMa Experimental Theatre Club.

Jack Hibberd's play *Three Old Friends* was the first play performed in the tiny space. Since that time the crowded intimacy of La Mama has provided welcome opportunities to a host of playwrights, actors, directors, technicians, film-makers, poets and comedians. La Mama's list of Alumni includes such names as David Williamson, Cate Blanchett, Jack Hibberd, John Romeril, Graeme Blundell, Barry Dickins, Tes Lyssiotis, Lloyd Jones, the Cantrills, Richard Frankland, Judith Lucy, Julia Zemiro, and Uncle Jack Charles, but just as importantly, it has provided a creative home and low-financial/high-artistic risk-taking environment for many thousands of lesser-known names who have become the backbone of the Australian theatre, film, television and comedy scenes across more than five decades.

La Mama is proud to have played such a crucial role in fostering the distinguished careers of so many established and emerging Australian artists.

I set La Mama up, as a space for writers and directors to perform in but also it was a space where people came, as audience, to participate in the creative experiment... Betty Burstall, 1987

La Mama Theatre—which on various occasions has been called headquarters, the shopfront and the birthplace of Australian Theatre—was classified by the National Trust in 1999.

The two-storey brick building is of State cultural significance because it has been occupied by La Mama Theatre...The building is indelibly associated with the performance arts and is a rare manifestation of an experimental theatre in Australia—National Trust Classification Report.

Happily, after a devastating fire in May 2018, our rebuilt La Mama Theatre was reopened in December, 2021, like a phoenix rising from the ashes.

During its nearly 60 years, La Mama has presented more than 2,500 shows. Current programming consists of:

LA MAMA PRESENTS: INC. EDUCATION AND ON DEMAND (FEB – MAY)

PLAY: SCRATCH, EXPLORATIONS, IMMERSE (JUNE – AUG)

PARTNERSHIPS: FESTIVALS, FRINGE, CULTURAL CONSERVATION, FARADAYS (SEPT – DEC)

Performances take place at La Mama headquarters, and at our second performance venue, La Mama Courthouse, 349 Drummond Street.

La Mama continues to be an open, accessible space, actively breaking down barriers to the Arts through diverse programs, creative initiatives, affordable ticketing, improved accessible amenities and a welcoming ethos, for performers and audience alike, that has developed over the past six decades.

La Mama is home to many and open to all.

For details of all productions and events, and bookings

visit: www.lamama.com.au

WRITER'S NOTE

As a regional playwright, the inspiration for this play came from a very real situation. Every week I would do my shopping at the local Woolworths. I watched one young woman become increasingly passive in her circumstances, letting go of her ambitions and becoming content with her lot. This ignited a hunt for many women in the same position, only to find that my 'deli girl' was just one of many women stuck in the same dilemma.

This is not just a story of women in regional Australia, it is a story for all women. *STUCK* asks, why do women pull other women down? How are women shaped by class expectations? Why is motherhood idealised? How can we change the story for the next generation of young women? The work goes to the heart of what it means to be a female living in a patriarchal world, it deals with the trappings of class, internalised misogyny and the #metoo movement.

The play also draws on my experience after having two children. This made me acutely aware of what financial dependence can feel like and how strongly women are shaped by the stories and expectations they grow up with. Yes, motherhood was beautiful, but it did come at a cost, one that I feel was not openly talked about.

Megan Twycross

WRITER'S THANK YOU

Heartfelt gratitude to the following people and organisations who helped bring this work to the stage. First and foremost, producer Kate Hancock who has been pivotal in making it all happen, you are my artistic rock. Susie Dee, for trusting in the idea from that very first conversation, your dramaturgy, your deft direction and your continued belief in me as a writer. Peta Brady, Eva Seymour, Caroline Lee and Lucy Ansell for your ideas in the early stage development. To the design team Lindy Macauley, Ian Moorhead, Amelia Lever-Davidson and Spencer Herd, what a privilege to have your creative mark on this work.

Creative Victoria, Jo Porter and Regional Arts Victoria, David Jones, Susan Jones, Lisa McLeod and the Fletcher Jones Family Foundations, Gwen and Edna Jones Foundation, Robert Salzer Foundation, Bronwyn Dunston and Auspicious Arts Projects, Meg Deyell and the Lighthouse Theatre, Warrnambool Theatre Company, and Currency Press. Friends who donated to the Australian Cultural Fund campaign. But most importantly, thank you to Caitlin Dullard, Myf Powell, Maureen Hartley and all at La Mama for championing my work as a regional artist. This play would not exist without your ongoing support.

As always everything is made possible by the loving support of my friends and my family: Janette, Darryl, Benny, Elsie and Louis and Lorna Mcleod.

DIRECTOR'S NOTE

Megan asked me some years ago to work with her on her new play, *STUCK*. After reading an early draft I immediately connected with the world she was creating. The play presents us with two characters, one old, one young, both nameless. They work in a deli. They slice, dice and serve. They share mundanities and their dreams. They confront each other's reality. At times it is a battlefield - cruel and judgemental, other times it's fun and full of acceptance.

Megan's use of language is highly stylised, lean, pared back, poetic, rhythmic and at times crude. And there are challenges. The many exits/entrances, jumps in time and the need to keep the underlying tension bubbling away throughout. Also, in our version, creative elements come into play: the subtle sonic world, the use of bold lighting and design choices, all these are there to help create meaningful and sustained dramatic tension.

STUCK digs into the social issues of motherhood and class but it also works on a metaphoric plane. Do we go along with what is in front of us and passively accept the status quo? Do we accept our 'lot' in life as it unfolds? Do we have a choice? A choice to change direction? Do we continue to dream of a better life, a different life or can we be content?

What makes this play so exciting is the way it challenges the idea of complacency and the notion of choice. What is it to be stuck? Stuck in a relationship, stuck in a thankless job, stuck in a particular place or phase. Do we choose to stay put, or do we want something more? It is so easy for an outsider to observe, be critical and to judge. But not so easy when you're in it, and you're stuck.

Susie Dee

PERFORMANCE STYLE, LANGUAGE AND TEXT

On a narrative level, *STUCK* follows Young One, who spends her gap year working at a local deli alongside Old One, a long-term employee who has been at the deli for over thirty years.

The play unfolds episodically rather than through a linear timeline. Moments of choreographed movement reflect the repetitive rhythms of deli work, shaping the pace and physical language of the piece.

Stylistically, the work draws on influences including Artaud, Brecht and Grotowski, alongside echoes of Shakespearean theatre. The deli bell— a nod to Samuel Beckett's *Happy Days*— controls the action, halting or propelling the characters forward.

The characters remain unnamed, referred to only as Young One and Old One. They address each other through nicknames— Young Thing, Goodfornothin, Fresh Meat, Goodforsomethin— reflecting the ways women are categorised and defined by appearance or perceived value.

Other figures are similarly labelled, including Sleazy Mr Pasta Salad, Flirty Only Dodoni, Old Lonely Three Hundred Grams of Jarlsberg, and a Tub of Hummus. These exaggerated archetypes draw on familiar social stereotypes to reinforce the play's feminist themes.

Language in *STUCK* is heightened and distinctly Australian — both raw and poetic. Through invented words and intensified rhythms, everyday speech becomes charged, allowing ordinary moments to carry deeper meaning.

For the premiere season, the minimal **set** comprises a tiled floor, benches, and plastic strip doors leading to a fridge or cold-room area. The persistent refrigerator hum, sharpening knives, and flickering lights create an atmosphere of foreboding, mirroring the characters' emotional decline.

STUCK invites audiences into an intimate world where personal struggle intersects with broader social forces. Rather than offering easy answers, the play holds space for reflection, examining the systems that shape identity, relationships and choice.

BIOGRAPHIES

MEGAN TWYCROSS

PLAYWRIGHT

Megan Twycross is a writer, teacher and performer based in Southwest Victoria, committed to bringing regional voices to the stage. In 2011, her first full-length play *Smudged* previewed at LaMama Courthouse and was the recipient of Under the Radar fund, allowing it to premiere at the Brisbane Festival. *Cluster*, Megan's first play for young people won the 2020 APT Regional Playwriting Award, a mentorship with director Susie Dee and was shortlisted for the 2021 MTC Cybec Electric Series. Her most recent play *STUCK* was developed as part of La Mama Explorations. It was selected for the 2026 VCE Drama Playlist and premiered as part of La Mama Presents in May 2026. Last year, Megan was the recipient of the inaugural Fletcher Jones Fellowship which allowed her to work as Griffin Theatre Company's Literary Assistant on the Griffin Award. Megan has spent the last five years as the theatre director for all-abilities arts organisation Find Your Voice Collective.

BIOGRAPHIES

SUSIE DEE
DIRECTOR

Susie Dee has worked extensively in theatre as a performer, devisor and director both in Australia and overseas for the past forty years. She has been the Artistic Director of Melbourne Workers Theatre (MWT), Union House Theatre (UHT) and Institute of Complex Entertainment (ICE), whose projects received many accolades for their ground-breaking site-specific work. Susie has a long history of directing plays by Patricia Cornelius – *Bad Boy, RUNT* (fortyfivedownstairs, La Boite Theatre and Sydney Opera House) *SHIT* and *Love*, both toured to the Venice Biennale Theatre Festival. Other directing highlights include *Animal* (Theatreworks and Dark Mofo) *Anthem*, (Performing Lines/Melbourne, Sydney and Perth Festivals. She often works with Fat Fruit: most recently directing *Fuck Christmas*. She was the recipient of the Ewa Czajor Memorial Award for female directors (a residency with Theatre Du Soleil, Paris) and in 2022 she received the prestigious Australia Council Award for Theatre. Susie has won numerous Green Room Awards for Directing, most recently for *My Sister Jill* (Melbourne Theatre Company) winning the Green Room Award for 'Best Director' and 'Outstanding Production' in 2023. Last year she directed another Cornelius work – *TRUTH* (Malthouse Theatre) and two works at HotHouse Theatre (*Rodeo Clown* and *I'm With Her*) and *Fair Punishment* (Browns Mart Theatre).

BIOGRAPHIES

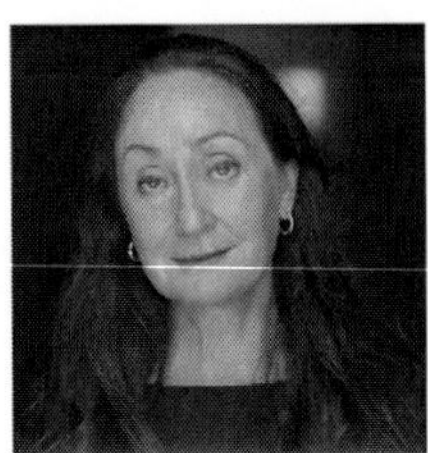

CAROLINE LEE

ACTOR

Caroline Lee is based in Melbourne, Australia, and has worked professionally as a theatre, television, film and voice actress for over thirty years. She has worked with many companies around Australia including the Malthouse, Sydney Theatre Company, Melbourne Theatre Company, Bell Shakespeare, Back to Back Theatre, Red Stitch Actors Theatre, Chamber Made Opera, MKA, Finucane and Smith, HeLD Productions, Hildegard, Playbox and La Mama. She is an ensemble member of the Red Stitch Actors Theatre, and has received three Greenroom Awards for Best Actress, as well as an OAM for services to the Performing Arts. Most recently she has played Lola Montez in *The Exotic Lives of Lola Montez* with Finucane and Smith, Honour in *Honour* (dir: Sam Strong), Rae in *Super* (dir: Emma Valente) and Aislin in *Your Name Means Dream* at Red Stitch (dir: Kat Henry); appeared in *June: a monologue about not speaking* by Patrick McCarthy (dir: Emily Tomlins) at Theatreworks; *Shhhh* by Clare Barron (dir: Emma Valente); and *Wittenoom* by Mary Anne Butler (dir: Susie Dee) at Red Stitch. Caroline is a well-known, and awarded, narrator of audiobooks, including such books as *Apples Never Fall* and *Big Little Lies* by Liane Moriarty. Film and television appearances include the role of Jean Pascoe in *The Newsreader* (series 1,2 and 3) and *Bogan Pride*; and roles in *Miss Fisher's MODern Murder Mysteries, The Dressmaker, Tangle, Winners and Losers, Satisfaction, Stingers, MDA, Halifax fp, Blue Heelers, Neighbours, Holidays on the River Yarra* and *Dogs in Space.*

BIOGRAPHIES

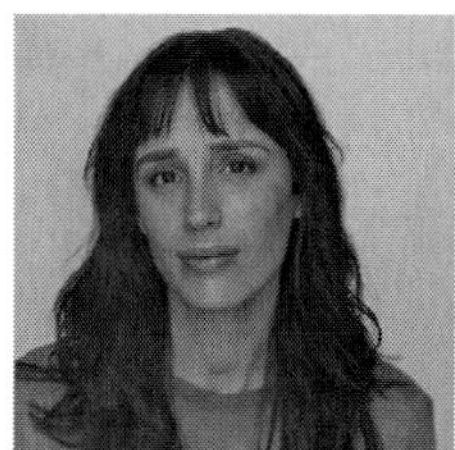

EVA SEYMOUR

ACTOR

Eva is an award-winning actor and writer working across screen, theatre and music. As an actor, she has worked with many theatre companies across Australian and UK. Notable works include *Truth* (Malthouse Theatre), *Puffs AU* (TEG Live) and *Anthem* (Performing Lines). Eva has also worked extensively on screen, in TV productions including *Dear Life* (Stan), *How To Stay Married* and *Neighbours* (Network 10). As a writer, her short films *Superstars* and *End Pointe* have screened at multiple Academy Award Qualifying Film Festivals across Australia. Her debut solo show *The Understudy* premiered at Melbourne Fringe Festival 2025, after which it won a weekly award for Best Theatre at Adelaide Fringe 2026. It continues to tour the festival circuit. Eva is also a published song-writer, having written for ARIA-award-winning artists Vika and Linda Bull.

BIOGRAPHIES

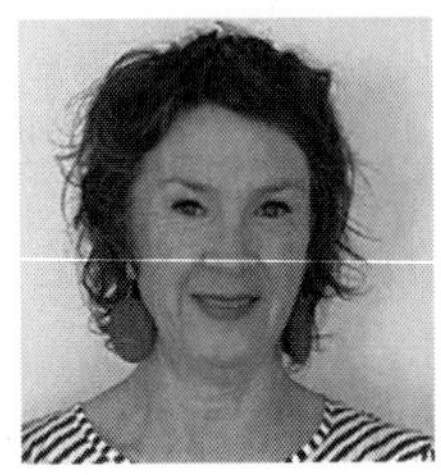

LINDY MACAULEY
SET & COSTUME DESIGNER

Lindy Macauley is a production designer based in Central Victoria, designing sets and costumes for theatre as well as facilitating visual art projects and curating exhibitions and events. She is a graduate of the Victorian College of the Arts Production Course and has worked on many theatre and visual arts projects as a designer, maker and curator She has worked with Arts Access Victoria, Melbourne Workers Theatre, Back to Back Theatre and Eleventh Hour as well as many independent artists. In recent years, she has worked as a visual art teacher and facilitator. In 2024, she returned to set and costume design, working on the productions, *Rodeo Clown* (Borderville Theatre, Albury) and *The Splendid Anomaly* (Arts House). In 2025, she worked as a design consultant for Hothouse Theatre's *I'm With Her* and *Where is Joy* (fortyfive downstairs).

BIOGRAPHIES

IAN MOORHEAD

COMPOSER

Ian Moorhead is a Melbourne (Naarm) based artist specialising in music composition and sound design for theatre, dance, circus, film and radio. He has performed around Australia and internationally, including New York, London, Edinburgh, Dublin, Wellington, Calgary and Vancouver. He has worked with numerous companies, including Melbourne Theatre Company, Malthouse Theatre, State Theatre Company of South Australia, New Working Group, Back to Back Theatre, Red Stitch Actors' Theatre, Dee and Cornelius, Windmill Theatre Co, Barking Gecko, Lab Kelpie, La Mama, Leigh Warren and Dancers, Patch Theatre Company, Restless Dance Theatre, Vitalstatistix, Circus Monoxide, NICA, Arts Centre Melbourne, Radiophrenia, Wave Farm, Ten Days on the Island, the Australian Festival for Young People, Underbelly Arts Festival, FOLA, Big West Festival, Darwin Festival, Museum Victoria, the Australian Museum and ABC Radio. He has been nominated for three Green Room Awards for his designs for *Jurassica* (Red Stitch Actors' Theatre in 2016), *Looking Glass* (New Working Group in 2018) and *Wittenoom* (Red Stitch Actors' Theatre in 2023).

BIOGRAPHIES

AMELIA LEVER-DAVIDSON

LIGHTING DESIGNER

Amelia Lever-Davidson is an award-winning lighting designer for theatre, dance, live art, installation, and events. Design credits include: *The Almighty Sometimes, Meet Me At Dawn, Bloom, Bernhardt/Hamlet, Girls & Boys, Slap. Bang. Kiss., Admissions, Torch The Place,* (MTC); *Macbeth (An Undoing), Hour Of The Wolf, Because The Night, K-Box, Australian Realness, Trustees* (Malthouse Theatre); *The Seagull, Julius Caesar* (STC); *The Wrong Gods, Blessed Union, My Brilliant Career, Every Brilliant Thing* (Belvoir); *They Divided The Sky* (Belvoir 25A); *Coriolanus* (Bell Shakespeare). Amelia's work has been presented nationally and internationally for Red Stitch Actor's Theatre, Chamber Made and Chunky Move, and at festivals including Noorderzon, RISING, DARK MOFO, Melbourne Festival, Now or Never, and Melbourne International Comedy Festival.

BIOGRAPHIES

KATE HANCOCK
PRODUCER

Kate Hancock is a producer with over 15 years of experience in the performing arts industry within Australia and the UK. For six years she was Executive Producer at Insite Arts International where she supported the delivery of large-scale events including Mona Foma (Tasmania) and Unsound Adelaide, alongside providing support for Insite Arts' stable of artists. This includes international presentations *Rooman*, theatre work by Fleur Elise Noble at the Busan International Performing Arts Festival (Korea) 2023 and *In Muva We Trust*, large scale outdoor projection work as part of the Fierce Festival/ Birmingham 2022 Commonwealth Games. Kate is currently producer at disability arts organisation Find Your Voice Collective.